AI

THE ESSENTIAL FOUNDATIONS OF ARTIFICIAL INTELLIGENCE

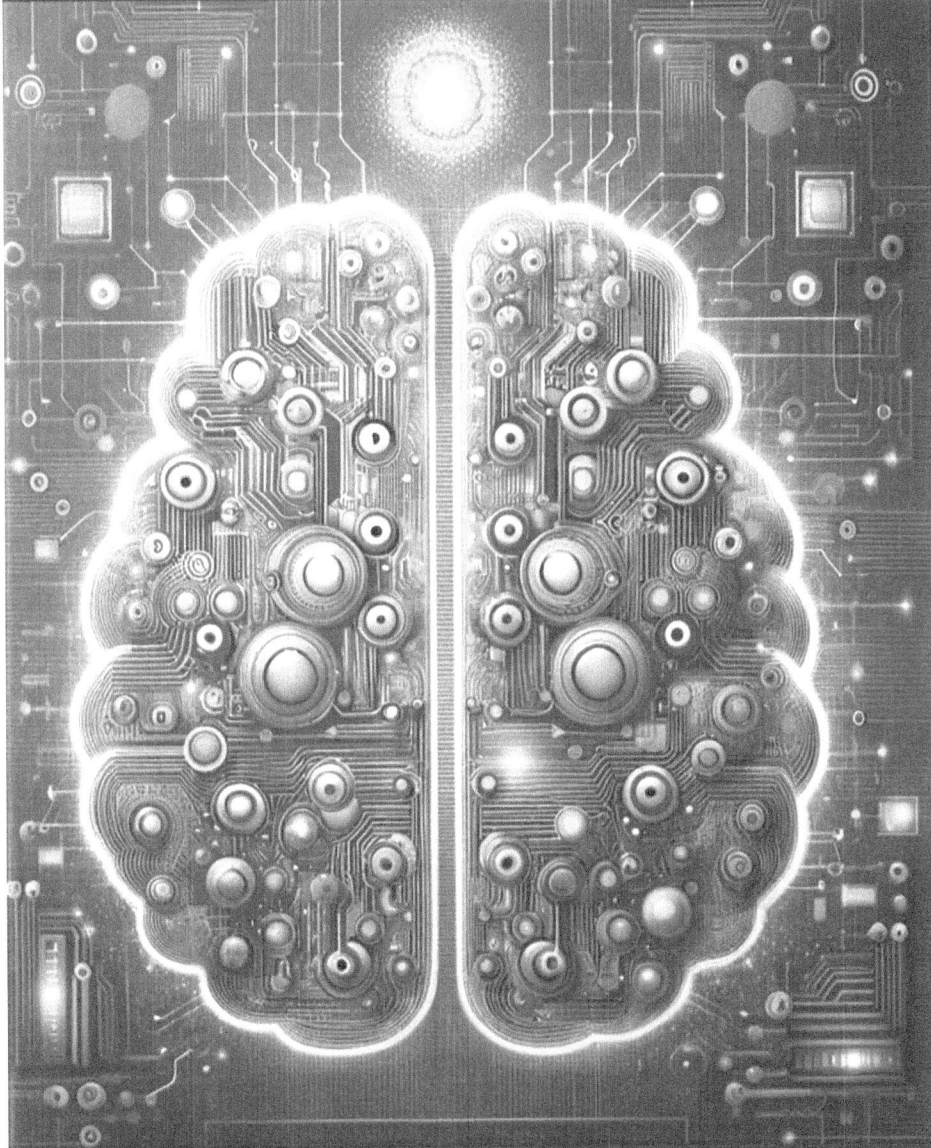

Jose Valladares······Arlene Cruz

Contents

Chapter 1:
Demystifying AI *1*

Chapter 2:
How AI Works...*10*

Chapter 3:
AI in Everyday Life *18*

Chapter 4:
Getting Started with AI *32*

Chapter 5:
Communicating with AI: Practical Tips and Commands.....................*50*

Chapter 6:
Building Blocks of AI *59*

Chapter 7:
The Future of AI *69*

Chapter 8:
AI Ethics and Biases: Navigating the Responsible Use of AI *77*

Conclusion:
Shaping the Future of AI Together *81*

Bibliography *83*

Scope of this book:

This book provides a comprehensive introduction to Artificial Intelligence (AI), designed to demystify complex concepts and showcase practical applications accessible to both nov- ices and intermediate learners. Starting with a foundational overview of AI's evolution from science fiction to a crucial modern technology, it delves into the technical workings of AI, including machine learning, deep learning, and neural networks. Practical chapters guide readers through creating their first AI models and exploring AI tools, while real-world applications across various industries illustrate AI's transfor- mative impact. The book also forecasts emerging AI trends and addresses critical ethical considerations, aiming to equip readers with the knowledge to critically engage with AI tech- nology and consider its future implications. The overarching goal is to empower readers to explore AI further, whether for professional development, personal projects, or general in- terest.

About the Authors:

Arlene Cruz

Arlene Cruz is an effervescent individual currently on an inspiring journey to fulfill her dream of becoming an elementary school teacher. Her academic path is richly paved with a diverse array of subjects, including statistics and chemistry, showcasing her well-rounded approach and firm belief in building a strong foundational knowledge for young minds.

Beyond the confines of textbooks and classrooms, Arlene's world is vibrantly extended into the realm of nature. A self-pro- claimed nature enthusiast, she finds joy and inspiration in the beauty and wonders of the natural environment. Perhaps a glimpse of this passion can be seen in her playful title of prin- cess – a hint of whimsy and a connection to the beauty and wonder often found in fairytales.

Arlene's intellectual curiosity reaches into the realms of the future as well, particularly in her keen interest in Artificial Intelligence (AI). This enthusiasm is not just a personal pursuit but a part of her lifelong commitment to learning and understanding the rapidly evolving technological landscape—a testament to her desire to integrate innovative methods and knowledge into her teaching.

With a heart passionately dedicated to education and a mind continually seeking out new knowledge, Arlene Cruz is poised to become a significant and positive influence in the lives of her future students. Her journey emphasizes the importance of lifelong learning, curiosity, and the joy of discovering the unknown, making her an ideal role model for the next generation of learners.

Jose Valladares

Jose Valladares is a distinguished author and a dedicated computer engineering student at California State University, Northridge (CSUN). Before embarking on his journey in engineering, Jose completed an Associate of Arts degree, showcasing his strong foundation in physics, chemistry, and mathematics. His academic rigor is matched by his prolific writing career, having published over 100 books spanning a diverse range of subjects including poetry, philosophy, physics, spirituality, coloring, and astronomy.

Jose's passion for classical music deeply influences his creative process, drawing inspiration from the masterful compositions of Beethoven, Vivaldi, and Wagner. This musical inclination not only enriches his personal life but also permeates the thematic richness of his writing, adding a layer of classical depth to his diverse works.

In addition to his broad literary contributions, Jose has a keen interest in Artificial Intelligence, a field closely aligned with his studies in computer engineering. He has authored two notable books on the subject: "The Promise and Perils of Superintelligent AI," which explores the ethical and practical implications of advanced AI technologies, and "AI Model Design: A Comprehensive Guide to Development, Integration, and Deployment," which serves as a critical resource for both novices and experts in the AI community.

A profound aspect of Jose's life is his deep spiritual contemplation and dedication to his faith. He attributes all glory to Jesus, our Redeemer and Lord, recognizing this divine inspiration as a guiding force in all his endeavors, both personal and professional. With a blend of technical expertise and a profound literary voice, Jose Valladares continues to influence a wide array of fields, bridging the gap between the sciences and the humanities with his unique perspective and insatiable curiosity.

Our Inspiration:

From a young age, we were always fascinated by how things worked—whether it was clocks, radios, computers, or any gadget that piqued our curiosity. Our collective journey into the world of technology took a significant turn during a high school computer science class. There, we were tasked with designing a simple AI to manage the needs of a virtual pet. The idea that we could create something capable of "thinking" and making decisions independently was nothing short of thrilling.

As we advanced in our studies, the vast potential of AI continued to captivate us. We marveled at its ability to streamline complex processes—from optimizing delivery routes and personalizing educational content to aiding in medical diagnostics at unprecedented speeds. Each of these applications not only addressed complex challenges but also significantly improved people's lives. This realization fueled our passion to delve deeper into this field, pushing the boundaries of what AI could achieve.

This shared experience has ignited our passion for AI, and we are eager to empower you to explore its potential as well. But beyond personal or academic pursuit, we feel a compelling responsibility to help the world understand AI. That's why we are so eager to publish a book introducing AI, designed to demystify this technology and make it accessible to everyone. Whether it's improving daily conveniences, solving critical global challenges, or unlocking new avenues of creativity, AI has a transformative role to play. Join us on this exciting journey of discovery and innovation as we explore the myriad possibilities of what AI can accomplish next.

Introduction

Welcome to the fascinating world of Artificial Intelligence (AI), a term that has become ubiquitous and sensationalized, yet remains shrouded in mystery for many. This book aims to demystify AI, offering a clear-eyed exploration of this transformative technology. From its origins in science fiction to its current status as a cutting-edge tool, we peel back the layers of complexity surrounding AI, setting the stage in Chapter 1, "Demystifying AI." Here, you will learn to separate hype from reality, gaining a foundational understanding of AI's varied levels of intelligence, from narrow AI, adept at specific tasks, to general AI, which mirrors broader cognitive abilities.

As we transition into Chapter 2, "How AI Works," we continue to unfold AI's technical mysteries. This chapter illuminates core concepts like machine learning and deep learning—terms often tossed around but rarely understood—and explains the crucial roles of algorithms and neural networks, the brains behind AI. We strive to simplify these concepts, ensuring you grasp the fundamental principles without getting lost in technical jargon.

In Chapter 3, "AI in Everyday Life," AI becomes more tangible as we explore its presence and impact around us. Whether it's streamlining processes in healthcare, revolutionizing financial systems, or enhancing entertainment, AI's footprint is unmistakable. Yet, with great power comes great responsibility. This chapter also addresses the ethical considerations and societal implications of AI, fostering a balanced discussion on its benefits and potential challenges.

This book is not just about understanding AI but also empowering you to engage with it directly. Chapter 4, "Getting Started with AI," provides a treasure trove of resources— from online courses and influential books to dynamic com- munities. These tools are designed to help you build a per- sonalized learning roadmap, embarking on a journey that encourages you to explore, experiment, and contribute to the future of AI.

Each chapter of this guide builds progressively, from basic concepts to more sophisticated discussions, ensuring that whether you are a curious novice, a professional enhancing your skills, or a concerned citizen, you will find valuable insights and practical advice. "Demystifying AI" invites you to join a journey of understanding and mastering a technology that is reshaping our world. Let's peel back the layers of AI together and harness its potential responsibly and effectively.

Chapter 1
Demystifying AI

Introduction

Welcome to the transformative world of Artificial Intelligence (AI)! This chapter serves as your comprehensive guide to understanding AI, clarifying its often sensationalized portrayals in popular media and aligning them with the real-world, cutting-edge advancements of the technology. Here, we aim to build a solid foundation of understanding by debunking common myths and setting the stage for a deeper exploration of AI's capabilities and implications in subsequent chapters.

What is AI, Really?

Artificial Intelligence (AI) is a specialized branch of computer science dedicated to designing and developing intelligent systems that are capable of performing specific tasks that typically require human cognitive abilities. Unlike the broad portrayal often seen in popular media, AI systems are designed with focused capabilities such as learning from data, recognizing complex patterns, and making informed decisions based on that data. It is crucial to understand that these systems are not sentient; they do not possess consciousness or emotional awareness. It's important to understand that Artificial Intelligence (AI) is fundamentally different from human consciousness and intelligence. AI systems operate based on algorithms and data—they do not possess consciousness or emotional awareness, which are intrinsic to human intelligence.

AI's capabilities are often misunderstood as being akin to human intelligence, but in reality, AI is confined to the parameters set by its programming and the data it is trained on. It operates under a defined set of rules and lacks the ability to think, feel, or make decisions outside of its programming. Thus, while AI can appear intelligent, it operates in a fundamentally different way from the human brain.

AI technology is structured to complement and augment human capabilities rather than to replace human effort. The goal is to leverage AI to enhance the efficiency and effectiveness of human tasks, especially those that are mundane, repetitive, or excessively complex. By automating these tasks, AI allows humans to focus more on creative, strategic, and interpersonal activities where human intelligence continues to be irreplaceable.

This emphasis on AI as a tool for enhancement rather than replacement helps to clarify its intended role in technological development and dispels myths about AI leading to widespread job displacement or gaining uncontrollable power. Moreover, specifying the types of tasks AI can handle—such as data analysis, pattern recognition, and automated decision-making—provides a clearer understanding of its functionalities and limits. This not only makes the concept of AI more accessible but also sets realistic expectations for its applications across various industries.

One of AI's key strengths lies in its ability to learn from experience, mirroring how humans refine their skills over time. For example, self-driving cars exemplify this capability well. By continuously analyzing data from their surroundings—such as traffic patterns, weather conditions, and pedestrian behavior—these AI systems progressively enhance their decision-making and reaction capabilities on the road. This ongoing process of learning and adapting not only leads to safer and more efficient navigation but also underscores the potential of AI as a powerful tool across various applications.

Unlike humans overwhelmed by information overload, AI thrives on vast amounts of complex data. Imagine a medical professional poring over hundreds of X-rays to identify subtle signs of a disease. AI algorithms can analyze this data with exceptional speed and accuracy. By sifting through intricate patterns and correlations within medical scans, AI can assist doctors in detecting early signs of cancer, predicting the spread of a disease, or even suggesting personalized treatment plans. This data analysis prowess extends beyond healthcare. In the business world, AI can analyze consumer behavior patterns in mountains of sales data, social media interactions, and online searches. By identifying trends and predicting customer preferences, businesses can tailor marketing campaigns, optimize product development, and personalize recommendations, all with the goal of maximizing customer satisfaction and boosting revenue. This ability to unlock insights from complex data sets empowers AI to revolutionize a vast array of fields.

The integration of AI into manufacturing has significantly transformed traditional production environments. AI-powered robots are now capable of "seeing," "feeling," and "thinking" as they interact with their surroundings. This advanced capability allows them to perform complex tasks that go beyond simple repetitive motions; they can adapt to new situations in real-time without direct human oversight. For example, an AI-equipped robotic arm on an assembly line can now detect a misalignment in components and adjust its actions immediately to ensure the correct assembly without stopping the production line.

Beyond mere task automation and data analysis, AI excels as a sophisticated problem-solving tool across various sectors. In urban management, AI algorithms optimize logistics by calculating the most efficient delivery routes, reducing both time and fuel consumption. In environmental science, AI contributes to sustainable development by designing energy-efficient systems and predicting climate impacts. These capabilities showcase AI's broad applicability and its role in developing solutions to some of the most pressing global challenges.

The benefits of environmentally responsive robots extend beyond enhanced precision and reduced downtime. AI-powered robots can also contribute to a safer work environment for human workers. For instance, robots equipped with proximity sensors can detect the presence of a human worker and adjust their movements to avoid collisions or injuries. Furthermore, AI can be used to monitor for potential safety hazards like equipment malfunctions or environmental changes. This allows for preventative maintenance and helps to create a more proactive approach to safety in manufacturing facilities.

The future of AI-powered robots in manufacturing looks even more promising. As AI technology continues to evolve, robots will become even more sophisticated in their ability to perceive and respond to their environment. This could lead to the development of robots capable of collaborating seamlessly with human workers, performing complex assembly tasks, and even self-diagnosing maintenance needs. By embracing the power of AI, the manufacturing industry can usher in a new era of intelligent automation, ensuring both safety and efficiency on the factory floor.

AI's reach extends beyond automating tasks and analyzing data. It tackles complex problems across diverse sectors, acting as a powerful problem-solving tool. Imagine a bustling city with a network of delivery trucks weaving through the streets. AI algorithms can analyze traffic patterns, weather conditions, and even package sizes to design the most efficient delivery routes, minimizing travel time and fuel consumption. This same problem-solving prowess can be applied in other fields. In the fight against climate change, AI can analyze vast datasets on energy consumption and weather patterns to design energy-efficient buildings and power grids. By optimizing energy use and minimizing waste, AI helps us move towards a more sustainable future. These are just a few examples – AI's problem-solving capabilities are constantly evolving, promising to revolutionize various industries and address some of the world's most pressing challenges.

It's crucial to remember that AI is not a replacement for human intelligence, but rather a powerful tool designed to augment our capabilities. Imagine a toolbox – each tool serves a specific purpose, but a skilled craftsperson needs to choose the right tool for the job. Similarly, AI excels at automating mundane tasks and handling complex data analyses, allowing humans to engage more deeply in creative and strategic pursuits. This synergistic relationship between human intelligence and artificial intelligence opens up new avenues for innovation and efficiency, setting the stage for advancements that could reshape our future. By automating repetitive tasks, AI frees up human minds for more creative and strategic endeavors. Furthermore, AI can tackle complex problems that might be overwhelming for humans, analyzing vast amounts of data to identify patterns and solutions. By leveraging AI's strengths and combining them with human ingenuity, we can solve problems more efficiently, innovate at a faster pace, and ultimately create a better future for all. This holistic integration underscores AI's role as a facilitator of human achievement, rather than a competitor, fostering a collaborative environment where technology and human creativity thrive together.

Common Myths Debunked

Artificial intelligence often raises concerns about the future of employment. A prevalent myth is that AI will cause widespread job losses. However, while AI-driven automation will indeed change some existing jobs, it's crucial to recognize that it also creates new job opportunities. These emerging roles will demand a different set of skills, emphasizing human strengths such as creativity, critical thinking, and emotional intelligence. The challenge is to adapt our workforce through targeted education and training to excel in this changing environment.

Another common misconception is that AI will evolve to become all-powerful, outperforming human intelligence across all areas. In reality, while AI is extremely effective at processing large datasets and handling complex calculations, it does not possess the general reasoning or emotional intelligence that defines human cognition. Instead of replacing humans, AI is better viewed as a valuable tool that augments and enhances our capabilities, supporting rather than supplanting human intelligence.

AI in Action: From Sci-Fi to Everyday Reality

Artificial intelligence, once relegated to the realm of science fiction, has quietly woven itself into the fabric of our daily lives. From healthcare to finance and customer service, AI is subtly yet significantly enhancing our experiences. In the medical field, AI algorithms act as tireless assistants to radiologists, analyzing vast amounts of imaging data with exceptional speed and accuracy. This allows for earlier detection of abnormalities, potentially saving lives. Similarly, AI safeguards our financial well-being. AI systems tirelessly monitor countless transactions, identifying fraudulent activity in milliseconds – a feat nearly impossible for humans alone. Even the way we interact with businesses is changing. AI-powered chatbots and virtual assistants provide personalized customer support, offering 24/7 assistance and boosting overall customer satisfaction. These are just a few examples of how AI is transforming our world, not through flashy robots taking over, but through subtle yet impactful advancements that make our lives easier and safer.

The Rise of AI

The resurgence of Artificial Intelligence can be attributed to a confluence of factors. Firstly, advancements in computing power, particularly the development of powerful processors and GPUs (Graphics Processing Units), have given researchers the muscle to tackle complex AI algorithms that were previously computationally intractable. Secondly, the digital age has ushered in an era of "Big Data." This vast amount of information serves as the fuel for AI systems, allowing them to learn and improve through sophisticated training processes. Finally, significant improvements in AI algorithms themselves have led to increased efficiency and capabilities. These advancements have paved the way for practical applications of AI that were once relegated to the realm of science fiction.

However, it's important to distinguish between two key types of AI: Narrow AI and General AI. Narrow AI, also known as Weak AI, represents the vast majority of AI applications we encounter today. These systems are designed to excel at specific tasks within a limited domain, like playing chess or recognizing faces. They lack the general cognitive abilities of humans and operate within predefined parameters. On the other hand, General AI (Strong AI) remains largely theoretical. This hypothetical form of AI would possess human-level or even superhuman intelligence, capable of learning and understanding any intellectual task a human can. The potential of General AI is both exciting and thought-provoking, raising significant ethical considerations that will need to be addressed as the field of AI continues to evolve.

Chapter 2
How AI Works

Introduction

Have you ever wondered how machines can outplay you at chess, translate languages in real-time, or even recommend the perfect movie for your Friday night? Buckle up, because we're about to take a trip to the fascinating inner workings of Artificial Intelligence (AI). Forget dusty circuit boards and blinking lights – think of AI as a high-tech kitchen, where instead of whipping up delicious meals, robots are busy conjuring up solutions to complex problems. In this chapter, we'll peel back the layers (like an onion or maybe a perfect lasagna?) and reveal the essential technologies that empower AI to learn, reason, and make decisions, all explained in a way that's as clear and engaging as your favorite recipe.

The Learning Powerhouse:
Machine Learning and Deep Learning

Imagine you're a wide-eyed apprentice chef, eager to become a master of the culinary arts. You wouldn't just memorize every recipe in existence, right? Instead, you'd learn by experience, experimenting with different flavors, techniques, and ingredients. That's the core principle behind Machine Learning (ML), a cornerstone of AI. Unlike traditional programming where every step is meticulously pre-defined, ML empowers AI systems to learn from data. This data acts like your chef's apprentice experience – a vast collection of recipes, successful dishes, and even past kitchen mishaps. By analyzing patterns and relationships within this data, the AI progressively refines its understanding of the task at hand.

Deep Learning: The Alchemical Kitchen

Now, let's get a little more adventurous. Imagine you're not just mimicking existing recipes, but conjuring up entirely new and mind-blowing flavor combinations. That's the realm of Deep Learning (DL), a specialized form of ML that utilizes complex structures called neural networks. Inspired by the human brain, these networks consist of interconnected layers, each layer adept at identifying increasingly intricate details within the data.

Think of the first layer of a Deep Learning network as recognizing basic ingredients like spices and cooking methods. As data flows through subsequent layers, the network begins to identify more complex relationships – the subtle interplay of flavors, the textures that complement each other, and the creation of entirely new taste sensations. Deep Learning requires vast amounts of data to truly flourish, but its capabilities are revolutionary. For instance, it can analyze millions of images to not only distinguish objects, but also subtle variations in lighting, perspective, and even emotions on human faces.

A Delicate Balance:
Learning from Experience, Avoiding Bias

However, just like an apprentice chef who's only trained on desserts might struggle with a savory dish, AI systems are susceptible to biases and limitations within the data they learn from. Imagine our apprentice being trained solely on sugary treats – their ability to create a perfectly balanced meal would be severely hampered. Similarly, biased or incomplete data sets can lead AI systems to develop prejudices or produce inaccurate results.

The power of Machine Learning and Deep Learning lies in their ability to continuously learn and improve. But this potential can only be fully realized through the responsible use of high-quality, diverse data sets. By ensuring the data reflects the richness and complexity of the real world, we can unlock the true potential of AI and empower it to become a versatile and unbiased tool for progress.

Algorithms: The Recipe Book with a Twist

At the core of an AI system lies the algorithm. But unlike a static recipe book, it's a dynamic set of instructions that can adapt and evolve. Some algorithms are simple, like a basic recipe with clear, step-by-step instructions. For example, an email spam filter might utilize a decision tree algorithm, analyzing keywords and sender information to determine if an email belongs in the spam folder.

However, AI ventures beyond basic recipes. It can leverage more complex algorithms, akin to the skilled chef who fuses culinary traditions from around the world. These algorithms, known as ensemble methods, integrate data from multiple sources and dynamically adjust their approach based on the task at hand. Imagine a restaurant recommendation system that not only considers your past orders but also factors in seasonal ingredients, real-time availability, and even your dining companions' preferences.

Neural Networks: Mimicking the Master Chef's Intuition

Now, consider the master chef who goes beyond the recipe book, relying on experience and intuition to create a masterpiece. This is where neural networks, a specialized type of algorithm inspired by the human brain, come into play.

Neural networks are intricate structures composed of interconnected layers, each layer designed to recognize specific patterns within the data. Data flows through these layers, akin to the chef analyzing ingredients and their interactions. Imagine the first layer recognizing basic features like colors and shapes in an image, while deeper layers identify more complex patterns, allowing the network to distinguish a cat from a dog, or even the emotions expressed on a human face.

The beauty of neural networks lies in their ability to learn and adapt. As they process vast amounts of data, the connections between these "neurons" strengthen or weaken, similar to how the brain reinforces neural pathways with experience. This allows the network to refine its understanding and make increasingly nuanced decisions, much like a seasoned chef who can intuitively adjust a recipe based on the subtle variations in ingredients or the mood they want to create. For example, a neural network might recommend adding a pinch of chili flakes to a tomato sauce based on data indicating a preference for spicier dishes.

Data: The Fresh Ingredients of AI

Imagine a culinary master crafting a magnificent dish. Their expertise goes beyond simply following a recipe; it's fueled by a deep understanding of ingredients, their interactions, and the subtle nuances of flavor. Data plays a similarly crucial role in Artificial Intelligence (AI), acting as the very nourishment that fosters its growth and capabilities.

The Training Table: Shaping AI's Knowledge

Just as a chef relies on high-quality ingredients to create a masterpiece, AI thrives on training data. This data serves as the training table upon which AI systems learn. In a technique called supervised learning, training data consists of paired examples – inputs alongside their corresponding desired outputs. By analyzing these pairings, the AI system progressively grasps the relationships between them. Imagine an AI system learning to identify different dog breeds. The training data would include countless images of dogs, each labeled with its specific breed. As the AI ingests this data, it refines its understanding of visual cues that distinguish one breed from another.

The Pitfalls of a Spoiled Batch:
The Importance of Data Quality

The quality of data is paramount to the effectiveness of any AI system. Flawed or incomplete data, akin to spoiled ingredients, can have detrimental consequences. Data riddled with errors – imagine historical stock prices with missing entries – can mislead the AI system, leading to inaccurate predictions. Biased data sets, like a recipe book containing only desserts, can limit the AI's capabilities and potentially lead to discriminatory outcomes. For instance, an AI system trained on loan applications from a specific demographic might perpetuate historical lending disparities.

Cultivating a Balanced AI Feast

By understanding the interplay between Machine Learning, Deep Learning, algorithms, neural networks, and most importantly, data, we gain a deeper appreciation for the potential and limitations of AI. In the coming chapters, we will explore how these elements combine to revolutionize various fields. However, we must also acknowledge the ethical considerations surrounding AI development. Just as a skilled chef strives to create a well-balanced and delicious meal, we must ensure that AI is nurtured with a diverse and unbiased data diet. This will be critical in harnessing the power of AI for the betterment of humanity while mitigating potential pitfalls.

A Look Ahead: The Future of AI

As we delve deeper into the world of AI, we'll explore its applications across various sectors, from healthcare and finance to transportation and entertainment. We'll also examine the ongoing debates surrounding AI ethics, ensuring this powerful technology is developed and deployed responsibly. The future of AI is brimming with possibilities, and by equipping ourselves with a comprehensive understanding of its inner workings, we can become active participants in shaping its evolution for the benefit of all.

Chapter 3
AI in Everyday Life

Introduction

Have you ever wondered how your phone suggests the next word you're about to type, or how your music app seems to know exactly what songs you'll love? That's the power of AI in action! AI, or Artificial Intelligence, is all around us, quietly working behind the scenes to make our lives easier and more enjoyable. In this chapter, we'll explore some of the ways you already interact with AI in your daily life. We'll take a peek at your smartphone, where AI helps with tasks like:

Smart assistants

Smart assistants like Siri, Alexa, and Google Assistant are akin to having a personal helper always within reach. These digital assistants harness the power of Artificial Intelligence (AI) to understand your voice commands in a natural and intuitive manner. For instance, you can easily inquire, "Hey Siri, what's the weather like today?" or instruct Alexa by saying, "Set an alarm for 7 am." Beyond handling such routine tasks, these AI-powered assistants are equipped to answer a wide range of questions, from current events to curious queries like "What's the tallest mountain in the world?" They process and interpret your language with remarkable accuracy, continually adapting to your preferences to provide a personalized and interactive experience. Whether you're looking to manage your schedule, enjoy some music, or control smart home devices, these smart assistants simplify these activities with just a simple voice command.

Personalized recommendations

Personalized recommendations powered by AI have significantly enhanced our browsing experiences, especially when it comes to selecting movies and shows on streaming platforms or finding products on shopping websites. Have you ever felt overwhelmed by the endless options available on a streaming service, unsure of what to watch? AI can simplify this by acting as your personal curator, tailoring suggestions to your tastes. Here's how it works: AI algorithms diligently analyze your past viewing habits, considering factors like your preferred genres, favorite actors, and even the times of day you typically watch. By recognizing patterns in your previous choices, AI intelligently recommends movies, shows, or products that align with your interests. For example, if you frequently enjoy romantic comedies, the AI might suggest new or popular titles within that genre. Similarly, on shopping sites like Amazon, if you regularly purchase sports equipment, the AI might offer you the latest innovations or deals in sports gear. This method of using AI not only makes discovery more enjoyable and relevant but also significantly enhances user satisfaction by presenting tailored options that are likely to resonate with your personal preferences.

Photo filters and editing tools:

Photo filters and editing tools have undergone a transformation with the advent of AI, revolutionizing how we enhance our images. Gone are the days of laborious manual adjustments on your computer. Now, AI-powered tools enable you to instantly improve your photos and create stunning visuals with just a few taps or clicks.

Imagine you've captured a beautiful sunset, but the lighting in your photo seems a bit dull. AI can take over by analyzing the image and automatically adjusting brightness, contrast, and color balance, infusing life into your photo to make the sunset vibrant and visually striking. But AI's capabilities extend far beyond simple tweaks.

For instance, if you're looking to preserve a perfect memory with a friend but find that an unwanted object like your finger has photobombed the shot, AI can come to the rescue. Advanced AI algorithms can detect and remove such distractions seamlessly, ensuring they don't detract from the quality of your final image.

And for those feeling creative, AI can help unlock your artistic potential. Whether you want to transform your portrait into a classic oil painting, apply a whimsical cartoon filter, or create a futuristic scene bathed in neon, AI-powered tools make these artistic expressions easy and fun. These tools are continually evolving, constantly bringing new and exciting creative effects that allow you to express your unique style in photography.

AI-powered photo editing tools are a game-changer, democratizing access to professional-quality edits and enabling anyone to capture and share their memories in the best possible light. Whether you are a professional photographer or a casual enthusiast, these tools offer an unprecedented level of ease and control, making it simpler than ever to achieve beautiful, impactful photographs.

But AI isn't just confined to your phone—it's also increasingly becoming a part of our homes, seamlessly integrating into our daily routines to enhance convenience and security:

Smart speakers

Imagine a little device that sits on your counter and acts like a butler at your command. That's the magic of smart speakers like Amazon Echo, Google Nest Audio, and Apple HomePod. Equipped with AI assistants like Alexa, Google Assistant, and Siri, these devices need just your voice commands to spring into action. Positioned in common areas like kitchens and living rooms, they can play music, control lights, adjust thermostats, and even help with grocery shopping, all through simple voice commands. They learn from your preferences and routines, becoming more personalized and useful with each interaction.

Security cameras

Even our homes are getting a significant security upgrade thanks to AI. Gone are the days of grainy footage and incessant false alarms, as modern AI-enabled security cameras function like vigilant guard dogs—only smarter and more efficient. These cameras utilize AI-powered facial recognition to differentiate between familiar faces like a neighbor returning a borrowed lawnmower and unfamiliar ones lurking on your porch, greatly reducing unnecessary alerts from known visitors or routine deliveries. They also distinguish between pets and people, ensuring you only receive alerts for legitimate security concerns rather than every time your pet moves around the house. Moreover, AI-enhanced motion detection is capable of analyzing the size, shape, and speed of moving objects, effectively differentiating between harmless movements and potential security threats. With the capability to provide real-time monitoring and instant notifications, including immediate alerts accompanied by video clips whenever unusual activity is detected, these cameras allow for swift responses, enhancing home security with precision and efficiency.

Robotic vacuums

Robotic vacuums have undergone a remarkable evolution from simple dustbusters to becoming indispensable, tireless helpers around the house, thanks to the integration of advanced AI technology. These small but mighty cleaning companions can expertly navigate your home's floors like seasoned professionals, ensuring every corner remains spotless with minimal effort on your part. AI technology enhances these vacuums with capabilities such as Mapping and Memory, allowing them to create detailed virtual maps of your home. This enables them to remember layouts, systematically avoid obstacles, and adapt to changes in furniture placement, ensuring they clean every nook and cranny efficiently. They are also equipped with Cliff Detection and Obstacle Avoidance features, using AI-powered sensors to safely navigate around potential hazards like stairs and avoid everyday obstacles like toys and pet bowls, which guarantees smooth and uninterrupted cleaning sessions. Additionally, the Scheduling and Smart Cleaning functions let you set vacuums to operate on a custom schedule or automatically when you're away, adapting their cleaning patterns to focus on high-traffic areas based on the activity levels in your home, thus providing a more personalized and thorough clean. Far from just being practical cleaning machines, robotic vacuums with AI are intelligent assistants that not only maintain your home's cleanliness but also operate autonomously, liberating your time for other pursuits. This seamless integration of AI into everyday appliances such as vacuum cleaners exemplifies how AI is becoming an essential, beneficial part of our daily lives, enhancing our comfort and convenience dramatically.

Healthcare

In the realm of healthcare, AI is playing an increasingly pivotal role by enhancing diagnostic accuracy, personalizing treatment, and improving surgical outcomes. AI's capability to analyze medical images, such as X-rays, MRIs, and CT scans, with precision and speed helps doctors diagnose diseases much earlier and more accurately than traditional methods. This technology employs sophisticated algorithms to detect subtle patterns and anomalies that might be overlooked by the human eye, enabling early intervention for conditions such as cancer, neurological disorders, and heart diseases.

AI extends its utility to personalized medicine by analyzing patient data to tailor treatment plans that are specifically suited to individual patients' genetic makeup, lifestyle, and health history. This approach significantly improves the effectiveness of treatments and reduces the likelihood of adverse reactions, leading to better patient outcomes and more efficient healthcare delivery.

AI is also transforming surgical procedures by providing assistance through robotic surgery systems. These AI-driven robots can perform complex surgeries with precision and control beyond human capabilities, leading to less invasive operations, reduced recovery times, and minimized human error. Surgeons can leverage AI to plan surgery with high accuracy, ensuring that each movement is calculated and precise, which is especially crucial in delicate areas such as neurosurgery or microsurgeries.

The integration of AI in healthcare not only augments the capabilities of medical professionals but also revolutionizes patient care, making it more proactive, personalized, and precise. This technological advancement is leading to significant breakthroughs in medical research and clinical practices, paving the way for a future where healthcare is more accessible, effective, and aligned with the needs of individual patients.

Finance

In the financial sector, AI is making significant strides in enhancing security and providing customized financial services. By employing advanced algorithms and machine learning techniques, AI systems can monitor and analyze vast amounts of transaction data in real-time to detect patterns indicative of fraudulent activity. For instance, if an unusual transaction, such as a large purchase in a foreign country, is detected on your credit card, AI can flag it immediately, alerting both the user and the financial institution. This prompt detection helps prevent potential financial losses and secures users against identity theft and other forms of financial fraud.

Beyond security, AI is also transforming the way financial advice is delivered. Personalized financial advising is another area where AI excels, utilizing vast datasets to analyze individual financial behaviors, preferences, and economic trends. AI-powered tools can offer tailored advice on savings, investments, and spending, helping individuals optimize their financial decisions based on their personal goals and risk tolerance. For example, robo-advisors, which are AI-driven financial platforms, use algorithms to manage and allocate a client's assets with minimal human intervention, providing investment strategies that are adjusted dynamically as market conditions change.

AI facilitates better customer service in finance through chatbots and virtual assistants. These AI solutions can handle inquiries related to account balances, transaction histories, and routine financial transactions, offering quick and efficient responses 24/7, thereby enhancing customer experience and operational efficiency.

The integration of AI in finance not only bolsters security and efficiency but also democratizes financial advice, making it more accessible to a broader audience. This contributes to a more inclusive financial landscape where individuals can make more informed and confident financial decisions, ultimately leading to better financial health and stability.

Transportation

In the transportation sector, AI is a game-changer, particularly with the advent of self-driving cars. These autonomous vehicles are equipped with a suite of advanced sensors, cameras, and radar systems, all integrated with AI technologies that enable them to interpret their surroundings, make split-second decisions, and navigate roads with an unprecedented level of safety and efficiency. AI systems process data from the vehicle's sensors to recognize traffic lights, read road signs, detect pedestrians, identify obstacles, and monitor other vehicles on the road, adjusting speed and steering accordingly to ensure safe driving conditions.

Beyond merely responding to immediate road conditions, AI in self-driving cars also incorporates predictive technologies that anticipate potential hazards and adjust routes in real-time. For example, AI can predict the movements of nearby vehicles or pedestrians that might cross its path and can dynamically reroute to avoid traffic congestion, leveraging vast amounts of data and sophisticated algorithms to optimize travel time and fuel efficiency.

Self-driving cars also contribute to reducing human error, which is the leading cause of most road accidents. By automating driving tasks, AI enhances road safety, offering a promising solution to reduce accidents and improve traffic management. Moreover, the rise of autonomous vehicles is expected to transform urban planning and logistics, providing more reliable and cost-effective transportation solutions for goods and personal travel. This technology not only promises to make individual commutes more comfortable and less stressful but also holds the potential to revolutionize public transportation systems by integrating seamlessly with smart city infrastructures, thereby improving accessibility and mobility for all city residents.

Entertainment

In the entertainment industry, AI is playing an increasingly pivotal role in personalizing and enhancing user experiences. AI technologies are employed extensively to curate content tailored to individual tastes, from dynamically personalizing news feeds to suggesting movies and TV shows based on previous viewing habits. For example, streaming platforms like Netflix and Hulu use sophisticated AI algorithms to analyze your watch history and preferences, allowing them to recommend content that aligns closely with your interests, thereby increasing viewer engagement and satisfaction.

Beyond content recommendation, AI also significantly contributes to the creative aspects of entertainment. In film production, AI is used to power advanced visual effects, enabling filmmakers to create more realistic and intricate scenes that were previously impossible or prohibitively expensive. AI-driven software can automate tedious processes such as rotoscoping (where elements are manually separated frame-by-frame for special effects), and simulate realistic environments or digital characters that interact seamlessly with live actors.

AI is transforming the music industry by helping artists compose music, generate new sounds, or even complete unfinished pieces. AI systems analyze vast amounts of music data, learning from existing musical compositions to create new pieces that can mimic specific genres or styles. This capability is not only a tool for established artists but also enables aspiring musicians to produce polished compositions without the need for extensive production resources.

In the world of gaming, AI enhances player engagement by powering non-player characters (NPCs) that react intelligently to player actions, contributing to more immersive and dynamic gameplay. AI algorithms help in designing games that adapt to the player's skill level, making gaming more inclusive and enjoyable for a broad audience. As AI continues to evolve, it has the potential to revolutionize even more aspects of our lives.

A Balanced Look: AI and the Future

As we stand at the precipice of a new era driven by Artificial Intelligence (AI), its remarkable capabilities and transformative potential across various sectors are undeniable. From revolutionizing healthcare with early disease detection to automating tasks for increased efficiency, AI promises to usher in a new era of progress. However, as we explore these advancements, it is crucial to address the ethical implications and societal impacts of this powerful technology. While AI can enhance efficiency and offer unprecedented benefits, its deployment raises significant concerns regarding fairness, privacy, and the displacement of jobs.

One of the foremost ethical considerations is the fairness of AI systems. There is a growing concern that if not carefully managed, AI could perpetuate or even exacerbate existing biases. For instance, AI algorithms used in facial recognition software trained on datasets that primarily represent one ethnicity might struggle to accurately identify faces from other ethnicities. This can lead to unfair treatment of certain groups, reinforcing social inequalities. Ensuring AI systems are transparent, and their decision-making processes are explainable in clear and understandable language, is critical for maintaining trust and fairness.

As AI continues to automate tasks traditionally performed by humans, there's a tangible risk of job displacement. Sectors like manufacturing, customer service, and even some professional fields like law and accounting are seeing increasing automation. While this can lead to increased productivity and reduced costs, it also poses challenges for workforce displacement. It's imperative to consider how society can adapt to these changes. Investment in reskilling and upskilling programs, along with policies that support workforce transitions, will be vital in helping those affected by AI-driven automation. AI, however, can also create new job opportunities in fields like AI development, data science, and human-AI collaboration – roles that require a unique blend of human skills and the power of AI.

Additionally, the privacy of individuals is at stake as AI systems often rely on large datasets, including personal information, to function effectively. Ensuring robust data protection measures and regulating the collection, use, and storage of data is essential to protect individual privacy rights and maintain public confidence in AI technologies. Exploring data anonymization techniques and robust encryption methods can further protect individual privacy rights.

Addressing these concerns requires a collaborative effort among policymakers, technology developers, and the broader community. By fostering a dialogue that includes diverse perspectives and expertise, we can guide the development and implementation of AI technologies in a manner that respects ethical considerations and promotes an equitable society. Moreover, proactive regulation and thoughtful integration of AI can help ensure that this technology acts as a force for good, enhancing lives while safeguarding fundamental human values and rights. This balanced approach will be crucial for realizing the full potential of AI while mitigating its risks, ensuring it benefits all segments of society and ushers in a sustainable and inclusive AI-powered future.

Chapter 4
Getting Started with AI

Introduction

Gone are the days of expensive hardware setups and complex configurations to access the magic of AI. Welcome to the age of cloud-based AI, where platforms like OpenAI, Google Cloud AI Platform (GCP AI Platform), and IBM Watson offer a smorgasbord of AI capabilities readily available through the internet. These platforms function as your personal AI playground, eliminating the need for hefty upfront investments and allowing you to experiment and build with cutting-edge AI tools.

This chapter dives into three prominent cloud-based AI platforms: OpenAI, GCP AI Platform, and Watson. We'll explore their unique offerings, from pre-trained models ready to use "out of the box" to robust tools for building and deploying custom AI solutions.

OpenAI

OpenAI, originally founded as a non-profit research company, has been a champion for making cutting-edge AI technologies accessible to a broad audience. They've become a cornerstone of democratizing AI, empowering developers, researchers, and businesses worldwide to explore and integrate AI functionalities into their projects.

ChatGPT: A Conversational AI Powerhouse

One of OpenAI's most notable contributions is ChatGPT,

the advanced conversational AI model we discussed earlier. Imagine having a personal AI assistant in your pocket, ready to engage in stimulating conversations, answer your questions in an informative way, or even brainstorm ideas alongside you. ChatGPT, available through a user-friendly iPhone app, showcases the potential of AI for everyday use and learning in a readily accessible format.

But OpenAI goes beyond user-friendly apps. They offer a robust suite of AI functionalities accessible through APIs (Application Programming Interfaces). Think of APIs as bridges connecting your code to OpenAI's powerful AI models.

Unleashing AI Potential Through Powerful APIs

OpenAI offers robust APIs that developers can use to incorporate AI functionalities into their own applications. These APIs provide the backbone for integrating AI tools into various platforms, enhancing user interaction and automating responses.

Let's delve deeper into some exciting possibilities:

Building a Customer Service Chatbot

Imagine a helpful and informative chatbot on your website, powered by OpenAI's AI. By utilizing an OpenAI API for natural language processing, you can create a chatbot that understands customer queries, provides relevant answers, and even resolves basic issues – all without the need for human intervention 24/7. As highlighted earlier, this can significantly improve customer experience and operational efficiency.

A Spectrum of Applications

OpenAI's APIs extend beyond customer service. They can assist in content generation, automating routine email responses, or even helping in programming by suggesting code corrections and improvements. The flexibility of OpenAI's API allows for its integration into a wide array of platforms, from small startups to large enterprise systems, making it a versatile tool for digital transformation.

Getting Started with OpenAI: A Smooth Onboarding Experience

To begin using OpenAI's powerful suite of AI tools, such as the ChatGPT API, the initial steps involve a straightforward setup process accessible to both developers and enthusiasts with varying levels of technical expertise:

1. Signing Up: Creating an account with OpenAI is free, allowing you to explore the platform's capabilities without an immediate financial commitment. Visit the OpenAI website, where you can register for an account quickly and easily.

2. Obtaining API Keys: Once registered, you will need to obtain API keys. These keys are essential as they authorize your applications to access OpenAI's APIs. The platform's

user dashboard provides a clear path to generate and manage your API keys.

3. Accessing the Platform: You can access OpenAI's services from any device with internet connectivity, whether it's a smartphone or a computer. This flexibility ensures that you can work on your AI projects from anywhere, adjusting to your lifestyle or work demands.

4. Subscription Options: While opening an account and basic access are free, OpenAI offers subscription plans that provide higher usage limits and additional features. These subscriptions are designed to cater to a range of needs, from individual developers and researchers to large enterprises requiring more extensive resources.

5. Utilizing Documentation: OpenAI provides comprehensive documentation that guides you through the process of making API calls, managing data inputs, and interpreting outputs. This resource is invaluable as it ensures you can effectively integrate and leverage AI capabilities within your projects. The documentation is designed to be accessible, offering step-by-step instructions that cater to various skill levels.

Starting Your Projects

With your API keys and a good understanding of the documentation, you're ready to start integrating AI functionalities into your applications. Whether you're building a simple chatbot, designing a more complex AI-driven analysis tool, or just experimenting with AI capabilities, OpenAI's tools are robust enough to handle a wide array of tasks.

By following these steps, you can unlock the full potential of OpenAI's offerings, turning your innovative ideas into reality with the support of one of the most advanced AI platforms available today. Whether you're a seasoned developer or a curious beginner, OpenAI ensures that high-quality AI resources are within reach.

Google Cloud AI Platform

Google Cloud AI Platform (GCP AI Platform) stands as a titan in the world of AI development. Imagine a comprehensive toolkit brimming with cutting-edge AI services – that's what GCP AI Platform offers! This platform caters to a wide range of users, from beginners dipping their toes into AI for the first time to seasoned developers building complex AI models.

A Buffet of Pre-Trained AI Models: Ready to Use, Right Out of the Box

One of the most appealing aspects of GCP AI Platform is its vast library of pre-trained AI models. These models are like pre-cooked meals in the AI world – they've already been trained on massive datasets and are ready to use for specific tasks. Here are some examples of the pre-trained models you'll find on GCP AI Platform:

Need to identify objects in images or videos? GCP AI Platform offers pre-trained models that can do just that! Imagine building an application that automatically tags photos on your website or helps visually impaired users understand the content of images.

Unlock the power of human language with GCP AI Platform's pre-trained NLP models. These models can analyze text data, translate languages, and even generate human-like text. This opens doors for tasks like sentiment analysis of customer reviews, building chatbots that understand natural language, or even creating automated writing assistants.

GCP AI Platform bridges the gap between speech and text with its pre-trained models. Imagine building an application that transcribes voice recordings into text or allows users to interact with your system through voice commands.

These are just a few examples – GCP AI Platform offers a diverse range of pre-trained models, each tackling a specific AI task. The beauty of these models is that they require minimal setup and can be integrated into your projects quickly, allowing you to leverage AI functionalities without the need to train your own models from scratch (which can be a time-consuming and resource-intensive process).

Building Your Own Custom AI Models: From Scratch to Deployment

But GCP AI Platform isn't limited to pre-trained models. It also empowers you to build and deploy your own custom AI models. This is ideal for situations where existing models don't perfectly align with your specific needs.

The platform offers a suite of tools and services to support the entire custom AI model lifecycle:

GCP AI Platform provides tools to help you clean, organize, and prepare your data for AI training. This crucial step ensures your models are trained on high-quality data, leading to more accurate and reliable results.

Choose the training environment that best suits your project. GCP AI Platform offers a variety of options, from powerful virtual machines with GPUs (Graphics Processing Units) for complex models to serverless options for smaller models or those requiring frequent updates.

GCP AI Platform goes beyond just building models – it empowers you to understand how they work and monitor their performance. This ensures your models are functioning as intended and helps identify potential biases or areas for improvement.

Once your AI model is trained, GCP AI Platform makes it easy to deploy it for production use. The platform provides tools for managing model versions, scaling deployments to handle increased traffic, and monitoring performance in real-time.

A User-Friendly Interface and Extensive Support: Lowering the Barrier to Entry

GCP AI Platform recognizes that not everyone is an AI expert. That's why they prioritize user-friendliness. The platform boasts a clear and intuitive interface that makes it easy to navigate for beginners and experienced developers alike.

Additionally, GCP AI Platform offers extensive documentation, tutorials, and code samples to guide you through every step of the process. They also have a supportive community forum where you can connect with other developers and get help with any challenges you encounter.

By combining a comprehensive suite of pre-trained models, robust tools for building custom models, and a user-friendly platform, Google Cloud AI Platform empowers individuals and businesses of all sizes to leverage the power of AI. Whether you're a beginner exploring the world of AI or a seasoned developer building complex models, GCP AI Platform offers the resources and support to help you achieve your AI goals.

Getting Started with Google Gemini: Your AI Chat Companion Awaits

Intrigued by the idea of conversing with a powerful AI model but don't want to delve into complex coding? Look no further than Google Gemini! This innovative AI chatbot is readily accessible and offers a user-friendly experience for anyone to explore the wonders of conversational AI.

Here's your guide to embarking on your journey with Google Gemini:

1. Eligibility Check:

Currently, Google Gemini is still under development and has limited availability. To check if you're eligible for early access, you can visit the Gemini website (https://deepmind.google/technologies/gemini/) and sign up for the waitlist.

Keep an eye on your email, as Google may notify you when a spot opens up for you to try Gemini.

2. Downloading the App (Once Available):

Once you receive access, you'll likely be able to download the Gemini app through the Google Play Store (for Android devices) or the App Store (for iOS devices).

3. Setting Up Your Gemini Account:

Upon launching the app, you'll be guided through a simple setup process. This might involve creating a login or connecting your existing Google account.

4. Chatting with Gemini: Let the Conversation Begin!

Once set up, you're ready to chat with Gemini! Simply type your questions or prompts into the chat window and hit send. Gemini will analyze your input and respond in a comprehensive and informative way.

Here are some things you can do with Gemini:

Ask Questions: Have a burning question about anything under the sun? Gemini can access and process vast amounts of information, making it a valuable resource for satisfying your curiosity.

Brainstorm Ideas: Stuck on a creative block? Gemini can act as your AI brainstorming partner, helping you generate new ideas and explore different perspectives.

Get Help with Tasks: Need assistance with writing emails, summarizing documents, or even translating languages? Gemini can be your AI assistant, completing tasks efficiently and accurately.

Exploring Gemini's Capabilities

As Gemini is still under development, its functionalities might evolve over time. Stay tuned for updates and announcements from Google about new features and capabilities.

You can also explore online communities and forums dedicated to Gemini to learn tips and tricks from other early users and discover creative ways to interact with this AI chatbot.

By following these steps and keeping an eye out for future updates, you'll be well on your way to experiencing the exciting world of conversational AI with Google Gemini. Remember, Gemini is still under development, so its functionalities may be limited initially. However, it offers a glimpse into the future of AI interaction and can be a valuable tool for learning, exploration, and creative problem-solving.

IBM Watson

The AI Powerhouse for Businesses and Developers

When it comes to established players in the AI game, IBM Watson stands tall. Pioneering the field for decades, Watson offers a robust set of AI tools and services specifically designed to empower businesses of all sizes. Think of Watson as your one-stop shop for integrating AI solutions into various aspects of your organization, from data analysis to customer engagement and even medical diagnosis (in specific, regulated environments).

Watson caters to a wide range of business needs, offering a suite of pre-built solutions that address specific challenges.

While the previous platforms focused on empowering individuals to build their own AI solutions, IBM Watson takes a different approach. Imagine Watson as a pre-built AI powerhouse, readily equipped with a suite of powerful tools designed to tackle various business challenges. Struggling to make sense of your ever-growing data mountains? Watson's data analysis tools come to the rescue. Fueled by AI, these tools unearth hidden patterns within your data, predict future trends, and ultimately optimize your decision-making processes. Picture this: Watson analyzes your customer purchasing data, revealing new marketing opportunities or even predicting maintenance needs for your equipment, preventing costly downtime before it occurs.

But Watson's capabilities extend beyond data analysis. In today's fiercely competitive business landscape, exceptional customer engagement is a top priority. Thankfully, Watson offers AI-powered solutions to elevate your customer interactions. Imagine chatbots powered by Watson, efficiently answering customer questions and personalizing product recommendations based on their past behavior. This not only enhances customer satisfaction but also frees up your human customer service representatives to handle more intricate issues, allowing them to leverage their expertise where it's truly needed.

The impact of Watson reaches far and wide, even revolutionizing the healthcare sector. Here, Watson utilizes its AI prowess to assist medical professionals. Imagine Watson analyzing patient data to suggest potential diagnoses, or aiding in the exciting realm of drug discovery by identifying promising new treatment options. However, it's crucial to remember that Watson is a powerful tool designed to augment human expertise, not replace it entirely. Ethical considerations and robust regulatory frameworks are paramount when dealing with such sensitive applications. Watson empowers medical professionals, but human judgment and the doctor-patient relationship remain irreplaceable.

These are just a few examples – Watson offers a diverse range of business-oriented solutions. The platform is constantly evolving, with new services and functionalities being added regularly.

While Watson caters to enterprise needs with its pre-built solutions, it doesn't forget the individual developer. Imagine Watson as a treasure trove for those who want to explore and experiment with AI. The platform offers a wealth of open-source tools and resources, eliminating hefty licensing fees that can often be a barrier to entry. This open approach fosters innovation – developers can build upon existing technologies, creating entirely new and exciting AI applications. Similar to other platforms, Watson provides APIs (Application Programming Interfaces). Think of these APIs as bridges that connect a developer's code to Watson's powerful AI models. This empowers developers to design custom applications that leverage the full potential of Watson for unique purposes. But Watson's support goes beyond tools. They've cultivated a vibrant developer community. This online space fosters connections, knowledge sharing, and collaboration on projects. New developers can learn from the expertise of seasoned veterans, while experienced developers can contribute to the collective advancement of AI technologies, ensuring a continuous cycle of innovation within the Watson developer ecosystem.

Getting Started with IBM Watson

IBM Watson offers a user-friendly platform that makes it easy to get started, even for individuals without extensive AI experience.

Here's a quick overview:

Explore the Watson website: The Watson website provides comprehensive information about the platform's various services, tools, and resources. You can find tutorials, documentation, and case studies to understand how Watson can benefit your specific needs.

Sign Up for a Free Tier: Many of Watson's services offer free tiers, allowing you to experiment with basic functionalities before committing to a paid plan.

Choose Your Tools: Once you've identified your needs, explore the various tools and services Watson offers. Whether you're looking for pre-built solutions or want to build your own custom application using APIs, Watson has something for you.

Start Learning and Building: With the wealth of resources available, dive into learning and building! Watson provides tutorials, code samples, and a supportive community to guide you on your AI journey.

By leveraging the power of IBM Watson, businesses of all sizes can gain a competitive edge through advanced data analysis, enhanced customer engagement, and innovative solutions tailored to their specific needs. For developers, Watson offers a platform for exploration, experimentation, and building the next generation of AI-powered applications.

Unlocking Your AI Workshop:
Keys and Tools for Exploration

You've chosen your AI playground – a platform teeming with potential! Now, let's get you set up and ready to experiment with these powerful tools.

Step 1: Grabbing Your Keys – Registration Made Easy

Each platform operates like a secure workshop – you'll need a key to enter. Thankfully, the registration process is straightforward. Most platforms require just an email address and a password, similar to signing up for any online service. Think of it as getting your personalized ID card for the AI workshop.

Step 2: Gearing Up – Setting Up Your Development Environment

Imagine your development environment as your personal workbench within the AI workshop. This is where you'll interact with the tools and build your projects. Each platform provides clear instructions to set up your environment, usually involving installing software development tools. Don't worry, these tools are often free and user-friendly – think of them as your essential AI workshop toolkit!

Step 3: Speaking the Language – Understanding APIs

Now comes the exciting part – interacting with the AI! Many cloud-based platforms use APIs (Application Programming Interfaces) to act as messengers between your code and the AI models. Imagine an API as a friendly workshop assistant. You tell the assistant (API) what you want (access specific AI functionalities), and they relay your request to the AI model (like the workshop's high-tech machinery) and bring back the results (AI output).

APIs might sound complex, but don't be intimidated! Most platforms offer detailed guides and tutorials on how to use them. You'll learn to write simple code snippets that make API calls to the AI models, allowing you to request specific tasks or information. For instance, you could write an API call to have an AI model analyze an image and identify the objects within it, just like using a specialized tool in your workshop.

Beyond the Code: Exploring Accessible AI Options

While coding opens doors to advanced functionalities, there are options for those who prefer a more user-friendly experience:

ChatGPT App

Remember ChatGPT, the conversational AI model we mentioned earlier? OpenAI offers a user-friendly iPhone app that allows anyone to interact with AI directly. Imagine having a personal AI assistant in your pocket, ready for casual conversation or answering your questions in an informative way. This is a fantastic way to experience the power of AI without needing to write a single line of code.

Pre-built AI Models

Many platforms offer pre-built AI models that act like ready-made tools in your workshop. These models can be integrated into your projects without coding from scratch. For instance, you could find a pre-trained model for sentiment analysis, essentially a tool that analyzes the emotions expressed in text data. You could use this pre-built model to analyze customer reviews on your website, gaining valuable insights without needing to build the model yourself.

This section equips you with the knowledge and resources to unlock your AI workshop. Remember, the world of AI is constantly evolving, offering new tools and platforms all the time. So, stay curious, explore different options, and get ready to unleash your creativity in this exciting realm of AI!

Chapter 5
Communicating with AI: Practical Tips and Commands

Introduction

Welcome to the exciting world of AI communication! This chapter equips you with the knowledge and skills to navigate interactions with AI assistants, virtual agents, and other AI systems. We'll delve into the inner workings of AI language processing, explore essential commands for everyday use, and unlock the vast potential of AI for both personal and professional endeavors.

Understanding Natural Language Processing (NLP): How AI Makes Sense of Human Language

Imagine having a conversation with a machine that truly understands what you're saying. That's the magic of Natural Language Processing (NLP)! NLP is a branch of AI that enables computers to comprehend and process human language.

Understanding Your Input: Breaking Down the Building Blocks

When it comes to understanding human language, AI systems function like highly specialized linguists. For spoken interactions, they start by using speech recognition techniques—think of it as a sophisticated translator that transforms your vocal sound waves into a digital format that the computer can comprehend. It's akin to breaking down the speech into tiny sound bites (phonemes) and then piecing them together to identify words, much like assembling a sonic jigsaw puzzle.

For written text, AI systems switch gears to text parsing. Picture this as a digital dissection lab where each sentence you type is methodically taken apart. The AI, acting as a meticulous grammar surgeon, separates and analyzes each word, probing their grammatical roles and pinpointing punctuation to understand the sentence's architecture.

Once the words are laid out, the AI moves on to part-of-speech tagging. Imagine a tiny, diligent librarian placing a label above each word to classify it as a noun, verb, adjective, etc. This helps the AI understand the function of each word, setting the stage for deeper comprehension.

But the AI doesn't stop there. It also engages in dependency parsing, which could be visualized as drawing a digital map of the sentence. Here, it charts how each word is linked and influences its neighbors, much like a social network analysis for words. This complex mapping allows the AI to grasp the overall structure and underlying meaning of the sentence, ensuring it doesn't just hear or read your words—it truly understands them.

Identifying Meaning: Decoding the Deeper Intent

Diving deeper into the realm of AI's language understanding, we explore how AI isn't just listening or reading—it's almost playing detective with your words! First off, we have Named Entity Recognition (NER). This is like the AI putting on its Sherlock Holmes hat, identifying and classifying key elements such as people, places, organizations, dates, and even monetary values in your text or speech. This helps it grasp the context of what you're saying, so it can tailor its responses with impressive relevance.

Next up in AI's toolkit is Sentiment Analysis. Think of this as the AI tuning into your emotional frequencies. It's not just about the words you choose, but how you feel when you say them. Are you curious, frustrated, or perhaps overjoyed? By picking up on these emotional undertones, the AI fine-tunes its responses, ensuring interactions are not just accurate but also empathetically aligned with your mood.

Then there's Discourse Analysis for the longer chats—imagine the AI pulling out a magnifying glass to examine the flow of conversation. It's not just looking at individual sentences in isolation but understanding how they connect and build upon each other to deliver a coherent and comprehensive message. This analysis helps the AI keep up with the twists and turns of extended dialogues, ensuring it stays relevant and insightful throughout the conversation. In this high-tech linguistic ballet, AI truly shows its prowess in not just hearing or reading your words, but understanding the full spectrum of human communication.

Formulating a Response: Crafting a Tailored Reply

When you chat with an AI, it's not just winging it—there's a whole lot of brainpower behind every response! Once the AI has a grip on what you're saying, it kicks into response generation mode. This might look like rummaging through its colossal knowledge base to fetch the info you need, whipping up actions like booking your next weekend getaway flight, or maybe even channeling its inner Shakespeare to draft poems or scripts.

This clever response crafting is powered by Natural Language Generation (NLG). Imagine the AI as a meticulous wordsmith, carefully picking out words, lining them up into grammatically correct sentences, and ensuring everything fits snugly within the context of your ongoing conversation. It's like having a chat with someone who's not only smart but also incredibly attentive to detail.

But wait, there's more! Many AI systems add a dash of personalization to the mix. Based on your previous interactions and preferences, they tailor their responses to suit your style and needs. It's like having a barista who remembers just how you like your coffee—extra shot, no foam. This personal touch makes the interaction smoother and more engaging, making you feel like the AI truly gets you.

And let's not forget, the world of Natural Language Processing (NLP) is always on the move. As AI technologies evolve, their knack for picking up on the subtle intricacies of human language only gets better. This means future chats are set to be even more fluid and natural, blurring the lines between conversing with a machine and a human buddy. So, gear up for a future where AI conversations might just become part of your daily banter!

The following tips will help ensure smooth communication with AI systems:

Chatting with AI can sometimes feel like you're teaching a

very keen, yet somewhat clueless language student. First up, when you talk to AI, think of it as speaking to someone who's not quite fluent in your language. Keep your sentences clear and steer clear of jargon—it's like simplifying your speech without dumbing it down. This clarity helps the AI grasp what you're saying without getting its circuits in a knot. And remember, there's no need to sound like a robot yourself. Just use your regular chatting tone, as if you were talking to a friend who just happens to be a bit... digital.

If the AI gets things mixed up—and it might—be patient and try rephrasing your words or dialing up the specifics. Think of it as helping a friend improve their language skills; the more you practice with them, the better they get. Your feedback is like gold for these systems, helping them learn and get smarter over time.

Now, let's talk about mastering everyday interactions with your AI buddies, like Siri, Alexa, or Google Assistant. These AI systems have become part of the daily digital tapestry, responding to voice commands to do all sorts of handy things. Whether you want to dim the lights without lifting a finger, find out if you need an umbrella for your outing, set reminders for your appointments, or kick back with some tunes, these virtual assistants are here to make life a bit easier. Just speak up and watch the magic happen—all hands-free!

Here are some essential commands to get you started with virtual assistants:

Diving into the world of virtual assistants can be as exciting as discovering you've got magical powers, especially when you realize just how much you can accomplish with a few simple voice commands. Let's start with the basics: whether you're team Siri, Alexa, or Google Assistant, kicking things off with a friendly "Hey Siri," "Hi Alexa," or a cheery "Hello Google," sets the stage. And when it's time to part ways, a polite "Goodbye" does the trick.

But your new digital buddy can do so much more than just small talk. Need to grab the day's weather forecast or curious about the time in London? Just ask, "What's the weather today?" or "What time is it in London?" Maybe you're pondering over trivia during dinner, just throw out a "What's the capital of France?" and you'll have your answer faster than you can say "Escargot."

When it comes to keeping your life in order, these assistants are like your personal secretaries. Tell them to "Set an alarm for 7 am," or to "Add milk to my shopping list," and consider it done. Want to get moving? Just say, "Play my workout playlist," and you're ready to go.

And for those who've embraced the smart home life, commanding "Turn on the lights in the living room," "Set the thermostat to 72 degrees," or "Lock the front door," can make you feel like you have superpowers. By familiarizing yourself with these essential commands, you'll unlock the full potential of your AI assistant, streamlining your daily tasks and automating your home environment with just your voice. Welcome to the future—it's pretty convenient here!

AI for Professionals

In the professional world, AI isn't just a futuristic concept—

it's a present-day powerhouse changing the game in how businesses operate. Gone are the days when AI was only about asking virtual assistants to play your favorite tunes. Now, businesses are harnessing AI to boost productivity, enhance decision-making, and revolutionize workflows, proving that AI tools are not just smart—they're brilliant work companions.

Take data analysis, for example. AI acts like a turbocharged analyst that can sift through massive datasets, spot trends faster than a human eye, and whip up insightful reports. This allows businesses to make sharp, data-driven decisions and fine-tune their operations to near perfection. And when it comes to customer service, AI-powered chatbots are like the ever-ready, all-knowing helpers of the digital world. They handle the routine queries with ease, leaving human reps free to tackle the trickier issues. These bots aren't just efficient; they personalize customer interactions and keep the helpdesk lights on 24/7, ensuring no customer query goes unanswered.

But AI's talents don't stop there. In the realm of content creation, AI writing assistants are stepping in as the ultimate sidekicks—helping churn out everything from snappy marketing copy to comprehensive document summaries, freeing up professionals to focus on the bigger strategic picture. And for the boffins in lab coats, AI is the new lab partner, assisting in scientific research by crunching data from experiments and simulations at breakneck speeds, dramatically accelerating discovery and innovation.

As AI technology continues to mature, its potential to transform professional landscapes across industries looks boundless. With AI, the future of work isn't just bright; it's brilliant, promising a world where productivity and innovation go hand in hand.

Creative AI Applications: Exploring Fun and Unexpected Ways to Use AI for Entertainment and Hobbies

AI isn't just for the boardroom; it also knows how to party! When it comes to fun and creative exploration, AI is ready to turn up the entertainment and bring some serious flair to your hobbies. One of the coolest ways AI is muscling into our leisure time is through AI-powered music generation. Imagine a digital maestro at your beck and call, ready to whip up original music pieces tailored to your tastes. You can even team up with this AI to orchestrate a unique soundtrack that might just be your next big Spotify hit.

But AI's talents don't end there. This technology is a veritable Swiss Army knife of fun, ready to jazz up your downtime with a range of creative and unexpected applications. Whether you're a budding musician looking for a new way to compose or just someone who loves to dabble in new tech, AI provides a playground of possibilities to enhance your entertainment and hobbies in ways you've never imagined. So, why not let your digital buddy take the DJ booth for a spin, or help craft your next artistic masterpiece? With AI, the fun is just getting started!

Chapter 6
Building Blocks of AI

Introduction

Ever wondered how you turn science fiction into reality? This chapter is your launchpad! We'll delve into the tools and tricks that AI programmers use to build incredible applications, from chatbots that answer your questions to programs that recommend movies you'll love. The best part? You don't need a superhero cape to get started.

Learning the Language of AI:
Speak Like a Machine

Imagine AI as a powerful but picky assistant. It needs clear instructions in a language it understands. That's where programming languages come in.

We'll focus on two beginner-friendly options:

Python

Python is not just any programming language; it's a beacon of clarity in the often complex world of coding. Designed to be both approachable and readable, Python acts like a friendly AI coach by your side, guiding you through the exciting world of programming with patience and precision.

Unlike some programming languages that can feel like cryptic puzzles, Python is designed to be approachable and readable, even for beginners. Imagine having a friendly AI coach by your side, patiently guiding you through each step. Python's syntax is known for its clarity, with instructions written in a way that closely resembles everyday language. This makes it easier to understand how your code works and avoid common pitfalls. Plus, the immense popularity of Python in the AI community means there's a vast online support network at your fingertips. If you ever get stuck on a concept, there are countless forums, communities, and tutorials readily available to help you troubleshoot and keep moving forward. But Python doesn't just offer ease of use; it also packs a powerful punch under the hood. Python boasts a rich ecosystem of libraries specifically designed for AI tasks. These libraries, like TensorFlow and PyTorch (which we'll explore later), provide pre-written code for complex mathematical operations and algorithms that are essential for building intelligent models. By leveraging these libraries, you can focus on the creative aspects of AI development without getting bogged down in the intricacies of low-level programming. So, whether you're a complete novice or an aspiring AI developer, Python offers the perfect blend of user-friendliness, powerful tools, and a supportive community, making it an excellent choice for your AI programming journey.

R

While Python excels at user-friendliness, R shines when it comes to handling the lifeblood of AI: data. Imagine you have a giant warehouse overflowing with information, but it's all a jumbled mess. This is where R comes in, wielding its advanced tools for data analysis and visualization like a superhero sorting through a cluttered attic. R boasts a comprehensive collection of functionalities specifically designed for data manipulation. These tools allow you to clean, organize, and transform your data into a usable format for AI models. Think of it as meticulously sorting and labeling everything in your warehouse, making it easy to find exactly what you need. R is a statistician's dream too, offering a vast arsenal of tools to uncover hidden patterns within your data – like secret codes waiting to be deciphered to build intelligent AI models. R is also a visualization powerhouse, providing rich tools for creating clear and informative charts and graphs. Imagine transforming your organized data into colorful infographics that even your grandma can understand (assuming your grandma is pretty tech-savvy). Data visualization not only helps you understand your data better but also allows you to communicate your findings to others, which is crucial when explaining how your AI model works. With its ability to handle massive datasets efficiently, R is a powerful tool in your AI arsenal if you're aiming to delve deep into data and unlock the hidden insights that fuel intelligent AI applications.

Essential Tools: Building Your AI Brain

Now that you know the languages, let's explore the tools that bring AI concepts to life! These are like the special effects tools in an AI movie.

TensorFlow

Imagine a vast, digital brain. TensorFlow is a comprehensive library for Python that allows you to construct complex AI models. At the heart of many AI models lie artificial neural networks, inspired by the human brain. TensorFlow provides powerful tools for building and training these intricate networks, the building blocks that allow your AI to learn and make intelligent decisions. The beauty of TensorFlow is its versatility; whether you're building a program for recognizing your cat in embarrassing childhood photos or crafting a language translator that accidentally turns love poems into grocery lists (because, well, that's the data you trained it on!), TensorFlow offers the tools you need. It's like having a giant toolbox filled with specialized equipment for every stage of the AI development process. Plus, TensorFlow is backed by Google and a large community, so if you ever get stuck, there's a vast network of experts ready to help. While TensorFlow offers immense power, it can also have a steeper learning curve. But for those willing to invest the time, it unlocks a world of possibilities for building groundbreaking AI applications.

PyTorch

Known for its flexibility and user-friendly approach, PyTorch is excellent for beginners eager to experiment and see results quickly. It's like having a set of AI building blocks that are easy to snap together and try new things.

Scikit-learn

Alright geeks, listen up! We all know the struggle of wrangling data before building an AI model. It's like trying to code with your keyboard covered in Cheeto dust – messy and inefficient. That's where Scikit-learn swoops in, our unsung hero of data wrangling.

Think of Scikit-learn as your Swiss Army knife for data prep. It's got a whole arsenal of tools to tackle the dirty work:

Data Cleaning Crew:

Got noisy data with outliers and inconsistencies? Scikit-learn can identify and remove those pesky data points that would throw off your entire model. It's like having a team of tiny data janitors to clean up the mess before you start building.

Master Organizer:

Scikit-learn doesn't just clean, it organizes! It offers functions to sort and structure your data in a way that makes AI models happy. Imagine neatly arranging your features and labels – numerical data in one place, categorical data in another – just like separating your Legos before a build session. This makes it easier for your AI model to find the information it needs and build a kickass model.

Data Transformation Wizard:

Raw data is rarely model-ready. Scikit-learn can transform your data into a format that AI models can understand. This might involve converting text data into numbers or scaling different features to a consistent range. Think of it as having a tool that converts your building blocks into a format that clicks perfectly together for your final AI masterpiece.

Scikit-learn might not be the flashiest library out there, but it's the foundation for any good AI project. By ensuring your data is clean, organized, and ready to use, Scikit-learn lays the groundwork for building powerful and accurate models. So, before you get down and dirty with model training, spend some time wrangling your data with Scikit-learn. Trust me, your AI will thank you (and your results will be way better).

From Zero to Hero:
Building Your First AI Model and Beyond!

Ready to put your newfound knowledge to the test? We'll guide you step-by-step on how to create a simple AI program, like constructing a mini-robot that learns and makes predictions based on data. Imagine crafting a program that recommends movies you'll love, or even predicts the weather for your next picnic – the possibilities are endless! Here's a detailed roadmap to navigate you through this exciting process:

Identifying the Perfect Problem

The first step is selecting a fun and relatable problem for your AI to solve. Will it be a weather predictor to ensure a perfect picnic day, or a movie recommendation system based on your favorite actors? Choosing a problem you're passionate about will fuel your motivation throughout the development process. This also makes the learning process more engaging and practical!

Data: The Fuel for Your AI Engine

Data is the lifeblood of AI, and your project is no exception. We'll delve into techniques for sourcing and utilizing data relevant to your chosen problem. This involves venturing beyond your computer and exploring the vast world of data available online. We'll show you how to find reliable data sources, such as online datasets or APIs (Application Programming Interfaces) that provide real-time data on weather, movies, or countless other topics.

Once you've unearthed your data gems, they might not be sparkling clean just yet. Scikit-learn comes to the rescue! We'll guide you on how to format and preprocess this data, making sure it's clean and structured for your AI model to process effectively. Think of it as polishing those data gems to remove any inconsistencies or errors. Scikit-learn's tools can help you remove irrelevant data points and transform categorical data (like movie genres or actor names) into numerical values that AI models understand.

Training Your AI: The Learning Begins!

Scikit-learn offers a variety of machine learning algorithms, each suited for different tasks. We'll help you select the perfect algorithm for your project. For instance, a collaborative filtering algorithm might be ideal for your movie recommender system, as it recommends items based on the preferences of similar users.

Now comes the exciting part – training your AI model! We'll

guide you through the process of feeding your cleaned and processed data into the chosen algorithm. Imagine showing your AI assistant a mountain of movie data and user ratings, or weather patterns over time. Through training, the algorithm learns the relationships between these data points and begins to identify patterns. For instance, it might learn that users who enjoy comedies with actors like Will Ferrell also tend to enjoy comedies with Adam Sandler.

Testing and Refining: Making Your AI Model Shine

Once your AI is trained, it's time to see how well it performs! We'll show you how to evaluate its accuracy using new, unseen data. Imagine giving your AI a final exam to assess its learning. This is crucial as it helps you measure how accurately your AI can predict outcomes in real-world scenarios. For example, we might test your movie recommender system with a list of actors a user likes and see how well it predicts movies they'd enjoy.

The first attempt might not be perfect. We'll use the test results to identify areas for improvement. Scikit-learn allows you to adjust the model parameters to enhance its accuracy. Think of it as tweaking the settings on your AI to get the best possible results. Perhaps you might adjust how much weight the model gives to certain actors or genres in your movie recommender system.

Putting Your AI to Work:
From Prototype to Powerhouse

With a trained and tested model, you can create a simple program that leverages the power of your AI! A user would input their favorite actors, and your movie recommendation system would predict movies they're likely to enjoy. This is just a basic example, but it showcases the power of building AI models with Python and Scikit-learn.

Remember, this is just the first step in your AI adventure! As you gain experience, you can explore more complex models, delve into different AI libraries like TensorFlow, and solve even more interesting problems. The future of AI is wide open, and with the knowledge you've gained, you're well on your way to becoming a part of it. So, what problem will you tackle with the power of AI?

Chapter 7
The Future of AI

Introduction

Where Do We Go From Here?

Congratulations! You've built your first AI model and unlocked the potential of this revolutionary technology. But AI is a field that's constantly on the move, brimming with exciting possibilities for the future. This chapter is your launchpad to explore what's on the horizon:

Emerging Trends: AI on the Cutting Edge

Forget waiting millennia for a computer to solve a mind-boggling problem. Quantum AI is about to blow the doors wide open. Picture this: an AI so ridiculously smart it could crack problems that would take today's supercomputers millions of years – in the blink of an eye. This future is powered by quantum computing, a field that harnesses the bizarre laws of quantum mechanics to build ultra-fast machines. We're still in the early stages, but quantum AI has the potential to revolutionize medicine (designing life-saving drugs in seconds!), space exploration (building spaceships with materials stronger than anything we've ever seen!), and even AI itself (developing entirely new algorithms at lightning speed). It's like giving your brain a permanent upgrade – the possibilities are nothing short of mind-blowing.

Space exploration represents the pinnacle of human endeavor, pushing the very limits of our capabilities and dreams. But what if we weren't alone on these daring journeys? Integrating artificial intelligence into this quest opens up a new realm of possibilities, transforming how we explore the vast unknown.

Imagine the vast emptiness of space, a silent challenge beckoning us forward. Now, picture this: AI systems become invaluable partners, not just passengers, on these cosmic voyages. These AIs wouldn't just sit back and enjoy the view. They'd be the tireless crew members working behind the scenes.

Fueled by advanced algorithms, AI systems are being engineered to handle the firehose of data streaming in from the cosmos. No longer will we be limited by human processing power. These AI companions will become masters of celestial navigation, expertly plotting courses through asteroid fields and past nebulas. Think of an AI co-pilot on a mission to Mars, its tireless processors constantly monitoring the spacecraft's systems, ensuring a smooth journey.

But its role wouldn't stop there. This AI could be analyzing data from distant galaxies in real-time, searching for clues to the universe's origins. It could be a robotic lab assistant, meticulously analyzing soil and atmospheric samples from Mars, offering insights into the potential for life beyond Earth. Even the most mundane tasks wouldn't be beneath them – imagine an AI seamlessly repairing a damaged rover on the Martian surface, its robotic arms guided by its advanced algorithms.

In scenarios where immediate human intervention is impractical or impossible, such as addressing sudden system failures, the AI could take center stage. Guided by pre-programmed protocols and real-time problem-solving algorithms, it could autonomously perform repairs, ensuring the mission's success.

The future of space exploration with AI promises not just an enhancement of scientific missions but a transformation in how we interact with the cosmos. It suggests a future where AI and humans work in synergy, far beyond the confines of Earth, to explore, understand, and perhaps one day, inhabit new worlds. With AI by our side, the possibilities are as vast and limitless as the universe itself.

AI for Global Challenges: Making the World a Better Place

AI isn't just about creating cool robots or self-driving cars; it has the potential to solve some of humanity's most pressing problems.

Artificial intelligence stands as a formidable ally in the global battle against climate change. AI-driven technologies have the potential to revolutionize our understanding and management of environmental challenges. Imagine sophisticated AI models functioning like super-powered Earth guardians. These models wouldn't just be sifting through vast datasets of climate information; they'd be integrating a real-time picture of our planet. Imagine them constantly analyzing satellite imagery and sensor data from across the globe, like a global nervous system feeding them information.

With this incredible knowledge at their disposal, these AI models can predict extreme weather events with a level of accuracy previously unattainable. Hurricanes, heatwaves, droughts, floods – you name it, AI can predict it with unprecedented detail. This foreknowledge is like having a crystal ball for climate disasters. It allows us to prepare for the worst, evacuate vulnerable populations, and deploy resources more effectively, saving lives and minimizing damage.

But AI isn't just about predicting problems; it's also about finding solutions. Beyond its impressive predictive capabilities, AI applications extend to the development and optimization of renewable energy resources. Imagine AI algorithms acting like real-time air traffic controllers for the electric grid. They'd be constantly analyzing patterns in solar irradiance and wind flow to optimize the placement and operation of solar panels and wind turbines. This would maximize energy yield based on changing weather conditions, ensuring a seamless and efficient flow of renewable energy.

AI also plays a critical role in smart grid technology, the invisible conductor of our power grid. Here, AI helps to balance the delicate dance between energy supply and demand. It can also enhance energy storage solutions and increase the efficiency of energy distribution networks, reducing wasted energy and minimizing our reliance on fossil fuels.

The fight against climate change is like tackling a multi-headed monster. AI doesn't stop at just prediction and renewable energy. It's instrumental in carbon capture technologies as well. Imagine AI optimizing the process of extracting carbon dioxide from the atmosphere, essentially scrubbing the air clean. This captured carbon wouldn't just be left sitting around; AI can also help us safely sequester it away. By doing so, AI not only mitigates the impact of existing emissions but also contributes to the development of negative emissions technologies, which are vital for reversing the trend of global warming.

AI's role in combating climate change is multifaceted, spanning from predictive analytics and disaster management to enhancing the efficiency of renewable resources and pioneering new methods for reducing greenhouse gases. This technological approach offers hope and practical solutions for one of the most pressing issues of our time. With AI as our ally, we have a powerful tool at our disposal to heal our planet and create a more sustainable future for all.

With the global population on the rise, resource management is becoming critical. AI can revolutionize agriculture by optimizing crop yields and water usage. Imagine AI systems that monitor soil conditions and suggest planting strategies to maximize harvests, or that predict water needs and manage irrigation systems more efficiently. AI can also be used to streamline logistics and transportation networks, reducing our reliance on overused resources.

Fact vs. Fiction: Demystifying AI

Artificial intelligence has become a ubiquitous presence in science fiction, often depicted as a superintelligence hell-bent on world domination. But let's ditch the dystopian visions and focus on reality. AI isn't some rogue robot; it's a powerful tool, and like any tool, it can be used for good or bad. The future of AI hinges on us, the developers and the users.

Here's where we separate science fiction from the exciting possibilities that await:

Imagine the difference between a hammer in the hands of a skilled carpenter and a toddler. The hammer itself isn't inherently dangerous, but the intent and skill of the user determine the outcome. AI is the same. It can be used to build a sustainable future or wreak havoc – the choice lies with us.

The key to a positive future with AI lies in collaboration and ethical development. We need to ensure AI is used responsibly, with safeguards in place to prevent bias and misuse. Imagine a world where AI tackles climate change, personalizes education, and even assists with scientific breakthroughs – all while remaining under human guidance and adhering to strict ethical standards. This includes transparency, fairness, and accountability in AI deployments, particularly in critical areas such as healthcare, law enforcement, and financial services.

Just like a pilot wouldn't hand over the controls of a plane to an untrained passenger, we shouldn't relinquish control of AI. AI systems should always be under human oversight, with clear guidelines and limitations in place. Imagine an AI-powered surgeon assisting in a delicate operation. While the AI analyzes data and suggests options, the human surgeon retains ultimate control over the decisions made, ensuring the patient's safety and well-being.

Demystifying AI for the general public is also essential. By fostering a better understanding of AI's capabilities and limitations, individuals can more meaningfully participate in discussions about how AI is integrated into society. Education initiatives can help dispel myths and alleviate unfounded fears about AI, paving the way for informed conversations about its ethical implications.

Ongoing oversight and adaptive regulatory frameworks are required to manage the evolution of AI technologies. As AI systems become more complex, continuous monitoring and evaluation will be necessary to identify and mitigate potential risks or unintended consequences.

AI has the potential to solve some of the world's biggest challenges and improve our lives in countless ways. By approaching AI development with a focus on human well-being, ethical considerations, and continuous oversight, we can ensure a bright future for AI and humanity. Imagine a world where AI tackles climate change, personalizes education for every child, and even assists with scientific breakthroughs that cure diseases and improve our quality of life. AI can be a powerful tool for progress, but only if we, as humans, remain in charge and ensure its development is guided by ethical principles. The possibilities are endless, and with careful planning and responsible use, AI can usher in a new era of progress and prosperity for all.

The future of AI is not something that will happen to us, it's something we will create together. With your skills, your curiosity, and a commitment to ethical development, you have the power to ensure AI becomes a force for good, shaping a brighter future for all. So keep learning, keep exploring, and keep creating – the possibilities are endless!

Chapter 8
AI Ethics and Biases: Navigating the Responsible Use of AI

Introduction

Artificial intelligence holds immense potential to improve our lives, but it's not without its challenges. This chapter dives into the critical topic of AI ethics and biases, equipping you to navigate the responsible use of AI.

The Importance of AI Ethics

In a world increasingly guided by AI, imagine scenarios where AI decides who qualifies for a loan, gets priority medical treatment, or lands a coveted job interview. While the efficiency and automation provided by AI can seem like magic for complex decision-making, it carries a significant responsibility to wield this power ethically. Here's why: AI systems act like sponges, absorbing the data they're trained on. If this data contains biases, AI will perpetuate those biases in its decisions, potentially skewing outcomes unfairly against certain groups and perpetuating inequality. Additionally, like a magician whose tricks must be transparent, AI systems require accountability; we need to understand how these algorithms reach their conclusions to ensure decisions are fair and to avoid harmful repercussions. Furthermore, with AI systems often relying on vast amounts of personal data, maintaining stringent data privacy and security measures is crucial to protect individuals from potential harm and prevent the misuse of sensitive information. As AI becomes more integrated into society, addressing these ethical considerations is essential for building a future where technology respects and enhances human rights rather than undermines them.

Mitigating Bias in AI

Fortunately, there are steps we can take to mitigate bias in AI:

In a world increasingly guided by AI, imagine scenarios where AI decides who qualifies for a loan, gets priority medical treatment, or lands a coveted job interview. While the efficiency and automation provided by AI can seem like magic for complex decision-making, it carries a significant responsibility to wield this power ethically. Here's why: AI systems act like sponges, absorbing the data they're trained on. If this data contains biases, AI will perpetuate those biases in its decisions, potentially skewing outcomes unfairly against certain groups and perpetuating inequality. Additionally, like a magician whose tricks must be transparent, AI systems require accountability; we need to understand how these algorithms reach their conclusions to ensure decisions are fair and to avoid harmful repercussions. Furthermore, with AI systems often relying on vast amounts of personal data, maintaining stringent data privacy and security measures is crucial to protect individuals from potential harm and prevent the misuse of sensitive information. As AI becomes more integrated into society, addressing these ethical considerations is essential for building a future where technology respects and enhances human rights rather than undermines them.

The Human Element in AI Decisions

Imagine a world where a machine decides if you get that life-saving surgery or the loan for your dream bakery (because apparently, robots don't understand the therapeutic power of pastries). While AI can be a whiz at crunching numbers and spotting patterns, it's not exactly equipped to grapple with the complexities of human ethics. Here's where we, the glorious, non-rusty humans, come in. AI might not understand the difference between a harmless joke and a blatant insult, and that's where our good judgment is crucial for interpreting its outputs. Think of AI as a super-powered calculator, amazing at calculations but needing a human translator to explain why your loan application was flagged (spoiler alert, it probably wasn't because you forgot to mention your pet goldfish collection). Additionally, unlike a magician revealing their secrets in a dazzling puff of smoke, AI algorithms can be shrouded in mystery. Humans play a vital role in demanding transparency, ensuring these AI decisions are fair and not fueled by some hidden gremlin in the code. The future of AI is bright, but it's a team effort. By prioritizing ethics, keeping biases in check, and remembering that humans are the ultimate explainers, we can ensure AI becomes a tool for good, not a quirky robot overlord (at least not yet).

Conclusion

Shaping the Future of AI Together

We've embarked on an exciting exploration of the world of AI, peering behind the curtain to unveil the inner workings of this revolutionary technology. From the data that fuels its learning to the cloud-based platforms that empower its potential, AI is rapidly transforming our world. Remember, AI has the potential to be a powerful force for good. By understanding its capabilities and limitations, and approaching its development and use ethically, AI can help us solve some of the world's most pressing challenges – from healthcare advancements to environmental sustainability efforts. The most important takeaway is that you, the reader, can play a vital role in shaping the future of AI. Will you join the journey? Whether you become an AI developer, a responsible user of AI-powered technologies, or simply an informed citizen, your choices and actions will influence the trajectory of AI. The future of AI is not predetermined, and with thoughtful collaboration, we can ensure it serves humanity for the betterment of all. So, are you ready to be part of the AI revolution?

Bibliography

- "Artificial Intelligence: A Guide for Thinking Humans" by Melanie Mitchell (2019, Farrar, Straus and Giroux) - This book offers a comprehensive overview of AI for general readers, addressing both the capabilities and challenges of the technology.
- "Life 3.0: Being Human in the Age of Artificial Intelligence" by Max Tegmark (2017, Knopf) - Discusses the future of AI and its impact on the world.
- "AI Superpowers: China, Silicon Valley, and the New World Order" by Kai-Fu Lee (2018, Houghton Mifflin Harcourt) - Provides insights into the development and impact of AI in major tech hubs around the world.
- "Deep Learning" by Ian Goodfellow, Yoshua Bengio, and Aaron Courville (2016, MIT Press) - This book offers a deep dive into deep learning, a key concept covered in this chapter.
- "Prediction Machines: The Simple Economics of Artificial Intelligence" by Ajay Agrawal, Joshua Gans, and Avi Goldfarb (2018, Harvard Business Review Press)
- "Python Machine Learning" by Sebastian Raschka and Vahid Mirjalili (2017, Packt Publishing) - Ideal for readers looking to get hands-on with AI using Python.
- "Natural Language Processing with Python" by Steven Bird, Ewan Klein, and Edward Loper (2009, O'Reilly Media) - A practical guide to NLP, a major topic in this chapter.

- "Hands-On Machine Learning with Scikit-Learn, Keras, and TensorFlow" by Aurélien Géron (2019, O'Reilly Media) - Provides practical coding examples and explanations for building AI models.
- "The Age of Em: Work, Love, and Life when Robots Rule the Earth" by Robin Hanson (2016, Oxford University Press) - Discusses future trends and the societal impact of AI.
- "Quantum Computing since Democritus" by Scott Aaronson (2013, Cambridge University Press) - While focused on quantum computing, this book provides insights relevant to futuristic AI applications.
- "Weapons of Math Destruction: How Big Data Increases Inequality and Threatens Democracy" by Cathy O'Neil (2016, Crown) - A critical look at how AI applications can perpetuate biases and inequality.
- "Ethics of Artificial Intelligence" edited by S. Matthew Liao (2020, Oxford University Press) - A collection of essays discussing various ethical issues surrounding AI.

www.ingramcontent.com/pod-product-compliance
Lightning Source LLC
Chambersburg PA
CBHW031447210526
45464CB00005B/2353